fast
fun &
easy
FABRIC BOWLS

Linda Johansen

5 reversible shapes to use
and display

C&T PUBLISHING

Text© 2003, Linda Johansen

Artwork© 2003, C&T Publishing, Inc.

Editor-in-Chief: Darra Williamson

Editor: Eleanor Levie, Craft Services, LLC

Technical Editor: Joyce Engels Lytle, and Eleanor Levie, Craft Services, LLC

Proofreader: Susan Nelsen

Cover Designer: Kristy A. Konitzer

Design Director/Book Designer: Kristy A. Konitzer

Illustrator: Kirstie McCormick

Production Assistant: Jeff Carrillo

Photographer: Diane Pedersen

Published by C&T Publishing, Inc., P.O. Box 1456, Lafayette, California, 94549

Library of Congress Cataloging-in-Publication Data
Johansen, Linda.
    Fast, fun & easy fabric bowls : 5 reversible shapes to use & display /
Linda Johansen.
        p. cm.
    ISBN 1-57120-239-0 (paper trade)
    1. Machine sewing. 2. Bowls (Tableware) 3. Quilting. I. Title.
    TT715.J595 2003
    746–dc21
                                                    2003010813

Printed in China

10 9

Acknowledgments

Jay Thatcher, "The wind beneath my wings"

Jay Johansen & Evan Thatcher, my joys and my creative consultants, always ready to give an honest opinion at a moment's notice

Holly Halley, who first instilled in me a love of sewing and creating

Gordon Halley, from whom I learned how to mentally take things apart and explain it to others

Shady & Mocha, my shadows & constant companions

Without these ladies—Sidnee Snell, Kim Campbell, Libby Ankarburg, Jan Clark, Donna Beverly, Cindy McNutt Kaestner, Marc Kemper, Wendy Yoder Holub—this book and much of my quilting journey would not have happened

Nena Bement, for all the rides to Fitness Over 50—"It is really wonderful to have such creative clever friends"

The shop owners & their staffs who have supported me in so many ways: Jessica Yorgey at Quiltwork Patches, Barbara Schreiner at BJ's Quilt Basket Laura Wallace Dickson at A Common Thread

Eleanor Levie—Now I really know why editors get so much praise – you deserve it, and more!

The warm, friendly, helpful & enthusiastic family at C&T Publishing:

Jan Grigsby, Darra Williamson, Gael Betts, Amy Marson, Mari Dreyer, Diane Pedersen, Kristy Konitzer, Kirstie McCormick, and Gailen Runge, plus so many more

And all my wonderful students
Thank You

Contents

Introduction

Creating art is one of the most rewarding endeavors I can imagine, and these fabric bowls *are* art. Don't, however, let the word "art" intimidate you. Even if you lack confidence in your artistic ability, you will be surprised at what you can create. There are no rules and no wrong choices, just easier ways to do things, and that is where this book will help.

My initial inspiration for fabric bowls came from a bowl I saw in a slide show at a class with well-known quilt artist Nancy Crow. I immediately went home and tried several methods to replicate that bowl—all without success. A few years later, I discovered Timtex™, a thick interfacing used in baseball cap brims. This discovery opened up a whole new world for exploring bowl shapes. Soon after, I developed some wonderful ways to use heavy cotton canvas fabric as a stabilizer. These two materials inspire such different shapes that I can't say which is my favorite.

These bowls really are fast, fun, and easy. I am an impatient person: I like instant gratification and am not prone to finishing what I start when things go slowly. (Sound like anyone you know?) But with the how-to's in this book and a few quilting tools you probably already own, you can make a bowl in an afternoon or evening. And easy? Yes indeedy! If you can use a sewing machine, you can make a bowl.

What makes the bowls fun? For me, it's the chance to combine beautiful fabrics, to stitch with gorgeous threads, and to shape a bowl to fit whatever mood I am in on a given day! I love the reversibility of the bowls–the sheer delight of popping them back and forth to show off both sides. In addition, the bowls are also fun to fill and enjoy, or give as gifts. I use them to hold my sewing threads for a particular project and to tempt my family with candy. One sits on our dining table, holding a large column candle in winter and fresh fruit or a flowering potted plant during the summer. I also display my baskets on the wall, secured with a pushpin.

To ensure the success of your bowl-making adventure, I recommend reading through All the Basics (pages 6–13), and then making both a Square Bowl (page 14) and a Round Bowl (page 20). Next, skim through the rest of the projects and variations and choose what appeals to you, or mix and match techniques to create your own original style. The medium is fabric: it's flexible, and you can be flexible, too. Give yourself permission to play. The important thing is to have fun!

Happy bowlmaking!

Linda Johansen

the bowls in brief

Whether you are a novice to sewing, or an expert quiltmaker, start here and get a good understanding of bowl-making from the outset.

To make a fabric bowl, you'll begin by creating a textile sandwich with your favorite cotton fabrics on the top and bottom—almost like a wholecloth quilt. In this case, however, the filler is a firm stabilizer, not batting. Sometimes you'll fuse the layers together, other times you'll quilt them. Your textile sandwich may be a square, circle, or other simple shape, usually with a reinforced center area to give your bowl a stable base. You'll make cuts into the textile sandwich and either remove these cut-outs and bring the cut edges together, or overlap the cut edges. Either way transforms a flat textile sandwich into a 3-D bowl! The rest of this book explains how to make any of five types of bowls, with all the step-by-step guidance you'll need to keep it fast, fun, and easy.

all the basics

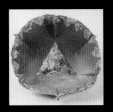

Here's a handy guide for choosing fabrics and materials, tools, techniques, and bowl shapes. Give it a quick read, then refer back here whenever you need some extra help.

Basic Materials
fabrics

For your first couple of bowls, it's best to use tightly-woven 100% cotton fabric—quilters' cotton. Your fat quarters are perfect, and scraps make great bases! The fabrics you combine for any one bowl should have something in common with each other, such as a color, theme, or mood. The more unique the fabric, the better!

Some Fabric and Thread Combinations

Once you have made a couple of bowls, expand your choices of fabrics. Consider home decorating fabrics, printed bed sheets, bandannas, cloth napkins, even stretchy, glitzy, or gauzy fabrics. Just avoid synthetics that would melt under the heat of the iron.

stabilizers

The sturdiness of a bowl is mostly dependent on the stabilizer you choose. There are two basic choices, referred to in this book as Timtex or canvas.

Timtex

Timtex comes pre-packaged or by the yard.

Timtex is ⅛"-thick interfacing made of rayon and polyester. It was developed by Thine (pronounced Tina) Bloxham of Timber Lane Press when she couldn't find the interfacing she needed for sewable, washable baseball-cap bills. Timtex is lightweight and holds its shape very well. Bowls made with it can be washed and shaped with steam pressing. Because this stabilizer is so thick, you won't need extra stitching to add firmness to your bowl.

fun!

Fuse scraps of fabric and Timtex together, and satin stitch around the edge to make a set of coasters!

You can purchase a package of Timtex—13½" x 22" (the minimum mail order for yardage as well). Or encourage your local quilt shop to buy a bolt (10 yards, 22" wide). Once you own some Timtex, you'll figure out how to make good use of the large leftover pieces by carefully cutting and zigzag-stitching pieces together along dart lines. Small scraps can be used to check stitches and thread tension. See the Sources on page 48.

fast!

Can't wait for Timtex? Substitute four layers of extra-heavy duty interfacing, pressing with fusible web between all the layers.

canvas

For more flowing, informally-shaped bowls, use "canvas" as the stabilizer. In this book, the term "canvas" refers to *any* heavy-weight, 100% cotton fabric, such as untreated canvas, denim, or duck fabrics. Be sure your chosen canvas is 100% cotton—otherwise the fusible may not stick to it, and the fibers of the stabilizer may actually melt under the iron. Look for fabric at least as heavy as the denim used in new, stiff blue jeans. The color of your canvas usually doesn't matter, although a black or other dark canvas may show through under a pale fabric.

Don't pre-wash your new canvas. If it has been washed, you can apply spray starch, as directed on the starch container.

When using canvas as a stabilizer, it's best to add dense lines of machine stitching to make the sides of the bowl firmer.

basting spray

For bowls made with canvas as the stabilizer, secure the textile sandwiches with temporary fabric adhesive, or basting spray. Use 505 Spray and Fix or Sulky Temporary Spray Adhesive, or any product that won't gum up the sewing machine needle. Follow the directions on the can, including taking the precaution of spraying where there's good ventilation.

Follow the directions that come with the fusible web.

easy!

Cover any mistakes on your bowl with fabric backed with fusible web (see Troubleshooting Tips, page 47).

fusible web

Fusible web holds the layers of a textile sandwich together and also adds stiffness to your bowl. In cases where you will be doing a lot of machine stitching through all the layers of the bowl, it is not absolutely necessary to use fusible web.

My personal preference for fusible web is Pellon® Wonder-Under™, but you can use any medium-weight product that fuses easily, has a paper backing that peels away easily, and holds well. Avoid the heavyweights designed for crafting; these are difficult to sew through and will gum up your needle.

thread

My thread of choice is usually a solid color or variegated cotton or rayon. Begin bowl-making with threads that work well for you. If you want to show off your fabric, select a thread that picks up a color in the fabric. If you want the thread to stand out as a design element, choose a contrasting color. For ease, use the same thread in the top of the machine and in the bobbin.

Use the same thread in the bobbin.

fun!

Try several types or colors of thread for the spiral quilting, then pick your favorite one for the darts and edge.

Basic Supplies

All of the "What You'll Need" lists for the individual bowls call for "Basic Supplies." This shorthand phrase refers to all those items you probably own for marking, cutting, pressing, and stitching. For cutting, you'll need rotary cutting tools and scissors; for pressing, you'll need an iron, ironing surface, and products to protect both of these from the residue of fusible web. For stitching, you'll need a sewing machine, presser feet, sewing machine needles—and a seam ripper, just in case! Continue reading if you'd like more complete explanations.

easy!

It pays to invest in the best quality tools you can afford. The process will go more smoothly and you'll be happier.

rotary cutter & mat

Your medium (45 mm) rotary cutter works fine. However, you may want to invest in a large (60 mm) rotary cutter so that you can make clean cuts—in one pass—through many layers of fabric, stabilizer, and fusible web. Also, for cutting Timtex alone, or shapes with curves and rounded corners, a smaller (28 mm) rotary cutter will provide greater flexibility. In any case, use the largest cutting mat you can afford.

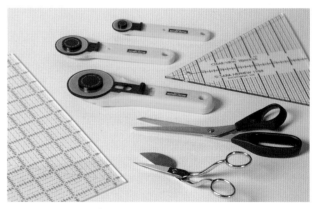

Cutting Tools and Supplies

scissors

To cut out angles such as darts, use a sharp pair of 6" fabric scissors.

Double curved, duck-billed appliqué scissors are very helpful for trimming excess base fabric close to the sewing line and trimming threads in or near the bottom of the three-dimensional bowl.

ironing supplies

Set your board to a height that is comfortable for standing. Use your iron on a cotton setting. It really pays to cover the top of your ironing board with a piece of inexpensive white fabric folded in half. You'll also want to put a pressing sheet under your projects whenever you are fusing the fabrics. I like the 18" square June Tailor™ pressing sheet for its size, speed in cooling, and ease of removing stray fusible adhesive.

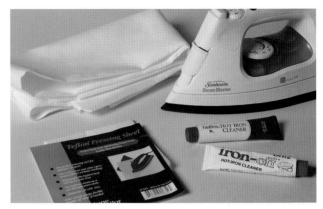
Ironing Supplies

easy!

Use the paper backing peeled off of fusible web to protect your ironing board. P.S.—My mom uses it for tracing paper!

Regardless of how careful you are, you'll probably get fusible adhesive on your iron. Then it's time to reach for a tube of hot iron cleaner. Squeeze the gel onto a heavy cotton cloth, and wipe that over the sole plate of the iron while it's hot.

Other Essential Supplies
marking tools

The How-To's for each bowl often specify that you measure and mark points, lines, or even curves. These markings will always be cut away or covered by stitching, so use what you have! I like mechanical pencils for their consistently fine lines. If you are planning on washing or steam-blocking the bowl, be sure your marker is permanent ink and won't bleed through.

templates

In tracing a shape onto materials, I rely heavily on a 12½" square, clear acrylic rotary ruler, and a 10" dinner plate from the cupboard. Many times I use the dinner plate merely as a guide, freehand rotary-cutting a few inches beyond the rim. Look around your home for larger serving plates or other objects that may serve as just the right template for your bowl.

compass

A good compass doesn't need to be expensive, just stiff enough to hold its span. You might want to use it to mark a perfect circle that's larger than your dinner plate. See page 11 for the Basic Techniques.

sewing machine & presser feet

Your sewing machine should be in good working order and able to zigzag and satin stitch in various widths. Refer to your machine manual and become familiar with changing upper thread and bobbin tensions.

An open-toe presser foot allows you to see what is happening and maintain good control while you sew your darts and side stitching. I use one almost exclusively, even for my regular sewing! If you like doing free-motion quilting, you'll need a darning foot as well.

fun!

Turn to page 47 for a mini-lesson on free-motion quilting.

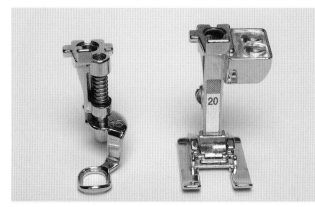

Darning Foot and Open Toe Foot

needles

Start every new project with a sharp, new needle in your sewing machine. Experiment to find the needle that works best for your choice of thread.

□ For a bowl made with Timtex, a 60/8 or 70/10 topstitch or Microtex sharp needle is a good choice. While it can be hard to thread the needle, it leaves only a small hole and provides a smooth-looking satin stitch.

□ For a bowl made with canvas, use an 80/12 topstitch needle or a Microtex sharp needle. Topstitch needles have a larger eye, a deeper slot up the back for the thread, and a larger shank for a bigger hole in the fabric. This mean less stress on the thread, so it'll be less prone to breaking or shredding.

□ If you are using several layers of a "canvas" such as denim, go up to a 90/14 topstitch or Microtex sharp.

□ Use a metallica or a metalfil needle for metallic or sliver thread.

Basic Techniques
marking

Use a compass to draw a circle larger than a plate at hand: Use a pin at the center and corners of the bowl layers. Center the plate face down on top. Set the compass for the extra width you need. Guide the anchor point of the compass around the plate rim, and mark a wider circle with the pencil. Cut along the marked line with scissors or a rotary cutter.

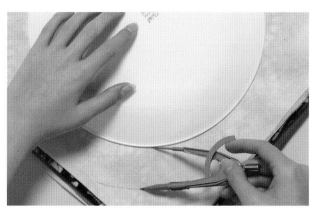

Use a compass to mark a circle larger than a plate.

cutting

You can do much of the cutting with a rotary cutter, slicing through all the layers at once.

However, cutting darts, snipping threads, trimming the edges of a base that's stitched down, or neatening up the edges of a bowl—all these call for scissors-cutting.

pressing & fusing

Iron your fabrics smooth before you use them in a bowl, and follow the manufacturer's instructions for the fusible web you are using. When applying fusible web, avoid getting the adhesive on your iron or ironing surface. See page 10 for products that protect these surfaces. *Note:* Always iron the fusible web to the fabric, then the fabric to the Timtex or canvas (which are too thick for the iron's heat to penetrate.)

creating darts

Just as darts shape clothing to the contours of your body, the darts in your bowl determine the contours. If you overlap the cut edges, the bowl will be stiffer and stronger. If you cut out the dart and butt the edges together, the bowl sides will be softer and more flexible.

Most of the projects in this book call for a specific dart shape. However, you are the creator of your bowl. Feel free to play. To empower your creativity, refer to the diagrams below, which suggest the general shape of bowl you can achieve from a specific type of dart.

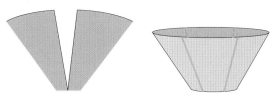

Straight darts produce a deeper bowl.

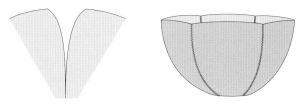

Use tapered darts for softly rounded bowls.

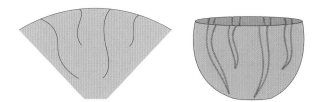

For uniquely shaped bowls, use secondary darts.

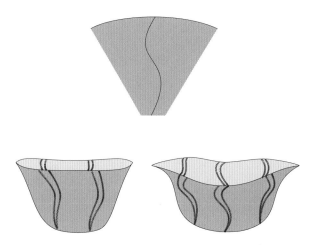

Curved darts add interest and shape to your bowl.

stitching

The purpose of the stitching (all by machine!) is to join edges, add stability to the sides of the bowl, and provide a design element. You will want the most balanced stitches you can achieve—stitches that look neat and even from both sides of your reversible bowl.

Check your stitching for correct thread tension every time you change from straight stitch to zigzag stitch or other decorative stitches. For a bowl with overlapped darts, make sure your machine can sew neatly through a double thickness of the textile sandwich.

fast!

Keep a small scrap of the textile sandwich you are using next to the machine to test for proper thread tension.

lock-stitches

To start and end off any satin stitches that won't be caught in subsequent lines of stitches, set your machine for the tiniest straight stitch—close to 0. Take a few stitches right alongside previous stitches. Clip the thread ends close to the surface.

easy!

If you forget to make lock-stitches, apply a dot of liquid sealant such as FrayBlock™.

decorative stitching

Contrasting thread can really add excitement to your bowl. Machine-stitch a pattern of stars, a grid, or continuous, concentric shapes on the base. If you enjoy free-motion quilting, or your machine does some fancy stitches, consider using a more interesting pattern. While decorative stitching can be done on the bowl at any time, it is easier to do—especially on the base—while the bowl is still flat. I add decorative stitching to the rim *after* I sew the darts.

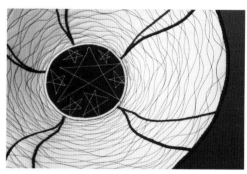

A simple pattern can make your bowl a star.

A triangular spiral adds a little pizzazz.

Use fancy machine stitches along the base and rim.

square bowl

Simple and showy, this project is perfect for your very first bowl—or your tenth one! Plus, you'll find that its bold, contemporary look offers lots of creative possibilities, proving that it is, indeed, hip to be square.

What You'll Need

- ☐ 2 fat quarters of complementary fabrics
- ☐ Optional 5" scraps for bases
- ☐ 1 yard fusible web
- ☐ 1 package, or ½ yard Timtex for the stabilizer (see the top of page 8 for a substitute)

- ☐ Thread to match or contrast
- ☐ Clear, acrylic quilter's ruler, 12½" square
- ☐ Basic supplies (see pages 9–11)

How-To's

cutting

1. Use a square ruler and rotary cutter to cut 12½" squares as follows: 1 from each fabric (for the 2 reversible sides of the bowl), 2 from fusible web, and 1 from Timtex (or a substitute stabilizer). For speed, layer the materials and rotary-cut them simultaneously.

Rotary-cut all the layers at the same time.

2. Cut 5" squares for the base on each side of the bowl: 1 from each fabric and 2 from fusible web. (You'll be trimming them down to 4" squares, so you can make do with slightly smaller scraps.)

fun!

Round the corners on your bowl by tracing around the edge of a spool of thread or around a cup.

fusing

1. Press your fabrics, so there are no wrinkles or fold lines.

2. Following the manufacturer's instructions, press a square of fusible web to the wrong side of each fabric square.

3. Peel away the paper backing on 1 fabric square. Center it on the Timtex square, and press to fuse. Repeat this with the second piece of fabric on the other side of the Timtex.

4. Trim the rather stiff textile sandwich carefully to a 12" square.

5. For the bases of the bowl, press one 5" square of fusible web to the wrong side of each of the 5" fabric squares, then trim each down to a 4" square.

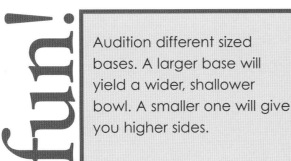

Audition different sized bases. A larger base will yield a wider, shallower bowl. A smaller one will give you higher sides.

adding the bases

1. Using a ruler and working on either side of the textile sandwich, mark a horizontal and a vertical line across the center. These lines will be cut out or covered up with stitching.

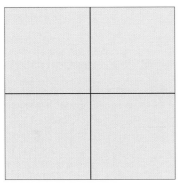

Mark lines across the center.

2. Position a fusible-backed 4" square, so 1 corner is on each of the marked lines. Press to fuse it in place.

Center 1 base over the marked lines.

3. Straight stitch just outside the edges of the base. Flip the textile sandwich over and position the second fusible-backed fabric square inside the stitched square. Press the second base to fuse it in place.

Straight stitch along the edges of the base.

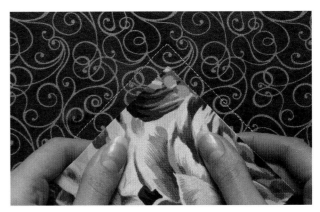

Position the second base inside the stitching.

4. Set your machine for a medium-width satin stitch. Check your tension on a scrap of the textile sandwich.

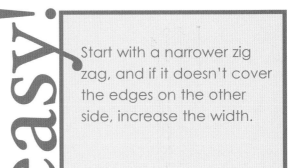

Start with a narrower zig zag, and if it doesn't cover the edges on the other side, increase the width.

5. Satin stitch around the edges of the base. Keep the center of the satin stitch along the edge of the base.

Satin stitch around the base.

shaping the bowl

1. Mark points on the edge of the textile sandwich, ½" on either side of the marked lines.

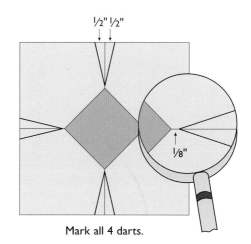

½" ½"

⅛"

Mark all 4 darts.

2. Connect these marks to a point ⅛" from a corner of the base. Repeat to mark a dart on each side of the large square.

3. Cut along the 2 marked lines, and remove the dart. Cut and then sew only 1 dart at a time, so there's less chance for the cut edges to fray.

Cut out 1 dart only.

4. Use the cut-out dart as a scrap to check the stitches and tension. Place the needle of your machine at the corner of the base, with the cut-out area in front of the needle. Begin zigzag stitching, moving toward the edge of the textile sandwich. The ⅛" between the base and the dart gives you a chance to adjust from a flat surface to one that's three-dimensional.

5. As you sew, pull the edges of the dart together in front of the needle, so the zigzag stitch catches both edges equally. Work slowly—if you try to pull the whole dart together when you start, you'll have puckering at the base of your dart.

Begin to sew the dart.

Pull the cut edges together as you stitch.

6. Continue stitching until you reach the edge of the textile sandwich. No need to backstitch—satin stitches along the edge will secure the thread ends. Cut and stitch the remaining 3 darts the same way.

easy!

If you're not happy with the shape of the bowl , you can change it. Simply cut through the stitching, recut the darts wider, then restitch them.

finishing

1. Set your machine for a slightly wider satin stitch. Sew over all the darts a second time, then satin stitch around the base again. Finish with lock-stitches (see page 13).

fast!

After you've made a bowl or two, do all the satin stitching on the first pass.

2. Use a medium-width satin stitch to sew around the edge of the bowl. The right side of the satin stitch should fall just beyond the edge of the fabric. Repeat with a slightly wider satin stitch. Finish off with a few lock-stitches.

Satin stitch all around the edge.

Almost **instant**
gratification!

Don't stop now...
dream up
another one!

Variations

Mixing and matching ideas, or making up the rules altogether—anything is fair and <u>square</u> in bowl-making. Consider the following options and more:

A. Quilt around the fabric motifs. Another possibility: leave the corners square.

B. Cut a triangle off each corner. Use a separate piece of pictorial fabric cut on the bias for each section of the bowl.

C. Start with a 14" <u>circle!</u> Use decorative stitching around the base and outer edges.

D. Two layers of canvas instead of Timtex give you a softer bowl with deeper darts and a sweetly curling rim.

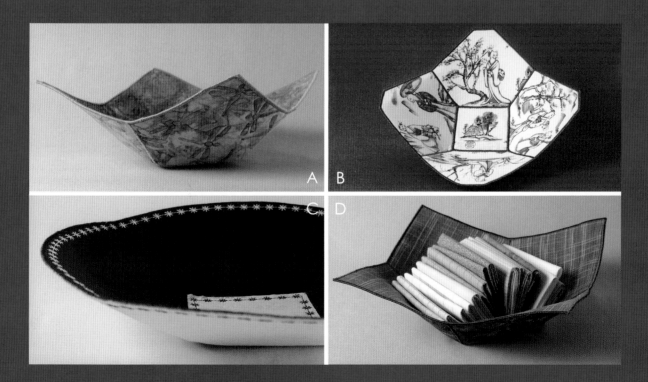

round bowl

With this wonderful project, even a novice will find herself rounding out a mastery of satin stitching and quilting by machine. Get ready—sharp-looking curves ahead!

What You'll Need

- [ ] 2 fat quarters of complementary fabrics
- [ ] Optional 5" scraps for bases
- [ ] 1 yard fusible web
- [ ] ½ yard of unwashed heavyweight canvas (see page 8)
- [ ] Thread to match or contrast
- [ ] Round dinner plate
- [ ] Compass
- [ ] Basting spray
- [ ] 90/16 topstitch needle
- [ ] Basic supplies (see pages 9–11)

Note: Be sure your machine can stitch through 2 layers of your chosen stabilizer plus 4 layers of your chosen fabric.

How-To's

making the textile sandwich

1. Stack the materials: Place the fabrics right sides together, and fold the canvas and fusible web so there are 2 layers. Insert pins to keep the layers from shifting. Place the stack on a cutting mat.

2. Set a round plate, bottom up, on top of the stack of fabric. Hold it firmly in place and use it as a guide for a circle. Use a compass to extend the diameter (see page 11), or pencil freehand, 1–2" beyond the edge of the plate.

easy! As you rotary cut, slide the plate around to keep the layers flat.

3. Rotary-cut along the extended circle (see the photo directly below), but add a small outward notch somewhere along the edge (see the bottom photo) so you can easily realign the layers.

Rotary-cut beyond the plate.

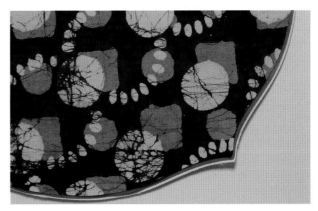

Cut a notch to help with realignment.

4. Remove the pins, and align the circles of fabric, fusible web, and canvas, using the notches as a guide. Fuse the web to the fabric, then the fabric to the canvas. Temporarily adhere the canvas layers together with basting spray.

adding the bases

1. Apply fusible web to the backs of two 5" scraps of fabric, and to two 5" scraps of canvas.

2. Use a compass to draw a 4" circle on the paper backing of the fusible web on just 1 of the canvas pieces. Cut this out with scissors.

3. Also cut out 1 fabric base, making it 1/16" larger all around than the canvas base.

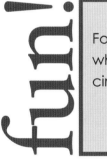

For your next round bowl, why not try a different size circle for the base?

4. Use a ruler to locate the exact center of the large textile sandwich. Fold the base into quarters, and lightly crease the point. Unfold and insert a pin from the fabric side at the center point. Remove the paper backing and insert the pin through the dot in the center of the textile sandwich. Keep the pin in place until you can smooth the canvas base out and press to fuse.

Center the canvas base on the textile sandwich.

5. Flip the textile sandwich to the other side. Peel the paper backing off the remaining 5" scrap of fusible-backed canvas. Use basting spray to temporarily adhere it in place, checking that it's centered over the first base.

6. Using a slightly shortened stitch length, straight stitch around the first, neatly cut base, keeping stitches 1/16" to the inside of the edge. Turn the textile sandwich over and trim away excess canvas beyond the stitches. Pull up on the fabric as you are trimming to get a nice close trim. Press to fuse the second canvas base in place.

A pair of double curved appliqué scissors helps you get as close as possible to the stitching and produce a nice, smooth edge.

Trim the second canvas base after stitching.

7. Repeat Steps 2-6 to apply the fabric bases. Satin stitch around the edge of the base. Your stitches should cover the edge of the base on both sides of the bowl.

Satin stitch around the base.

quilting the surface

1. Before you start shaping the bowl, quilt the base. This holds the layers together and makes the base firmer and more stable. Use a straight-stitch design such as one of the ones shown at upper right for inspiration, or consider free-motion quilting (see page 47). End your stitches with a few lock-stitches at an edge or along previous stitches.

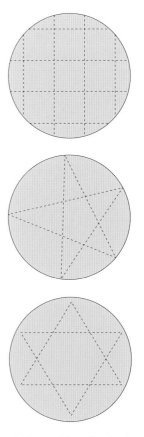

Straight-Stitch Design Ideas for the Base Patterns

2. For the sides of the bowl, set your machine for a slightly shorter straight stitch. Make lock-stitches alongside the satin stitches around the base, then straight stitch in an ever-widening spiral toward the outer edge. Gently shift the textile sandwich back and forth as you sew around and around to produce wavy stitching lines, crossing lines randomly as you go.

Sew in a random spiral.

shaping the bowl

1. The steepness of your bowl sides will depend on two things: the number of darts and how much you overlap each dart. (See Creating Darts, page 12.)

For your first round bowl, mark 6 darts by inserting 6 pins spaced fairly evenly around the base and/or the edges of your sandwich.

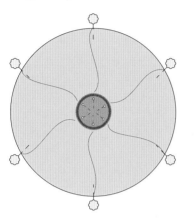

Note: Dart lines are imaginary only!

2. Here comes the scariest part for most first-time bowl-makers! Using scissors, cut a gently curving line from 1 pin along the outer edge of your unshaped bowl to within about ¼" of the base. Refer to the diagram, but cut only *1* curvy line. You'll be creating an overlap for this dart, not removing it, and you'll stitch along only 1 edge of the first dart before you cut the next dart.

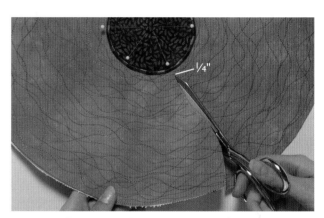

Cut the first dart; stop ¼" from the base.

3. Set your sewing machine for a very open zigzag. Slide the textile sandwich under the presser foot of your machine so that you are sewing from the base toward the outer edge. Start sewing before the dart actually starts. This eases the transition from flat sandwich to three-dimensional bowl. Sew along the dart, overlapping the cut edges slightly at the start, then increasingly to about 1" at the outer edge. You may need to hold the dart together close to where you are sewing. Keep the overlap smooth, and the zigzag stitch centered over the cut edge of the fabric.

Begin stitching before the cut dart.

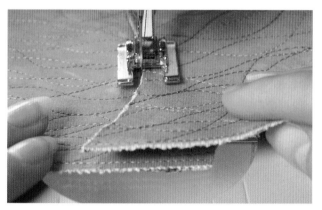

As you stitch, increase the overlap.

fun!

Want the lip to flare out a bit? As you approach the outer edge, gently pull the dart apart.

4. Repeat Steps 2 and 3 until you have cut and zigzag stitched 1 side of each dart. If you like the bowl shape, continue merrily along. If you don't, use a seam ripper to rip out the stitches of 1 or more darts and re-sew it.

5. Flip the bowl to the reverse side, and satin stitch along the other edge of the cut darts.

6. For a more finished look, satin stitch over all darts a second time. Secure the beginning of each line of stitches with backstitches or lock-stitches.

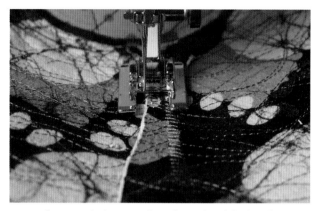

Satin stitch darts on the other side of the bowl.

fun!

Use a narrower stitch when you begin each dart, and graduate to a wider stitch at the outer edge.

finishing

1. Using scissors, trim the outer edge of the bowl so none of the bare canvas is showing and the bowl edge has the shape you want.

2. Satin stitch around the rim twice. For a wavy rim, tug on the fabric as you stitch the edge. For the first round, use a medium-width stitch; for the second time around, use a slightly wider satin stitch.

3. End your stitching with a few lock-stitches.

When everyone **admires** your artful bowl, don't admit **how easy** it was to make!

Variations

When you get a-*round* to trying something a little different, you'll find these techniques a cinch to do.

A. If you can draw a five-pointed star, you can give the base a starring role, with straight machine-stitching.

B. For a deeper bowl, add more darts, but cut them only half as long as the original darts.

C. Let your bowl sprout satin leaves. Adhere them with a bit of fabric glue, then secure them with stitching.

D. Take a rest from all that satin stitching with a sawtooth edging. Refer to page 34 for complete how-to's.

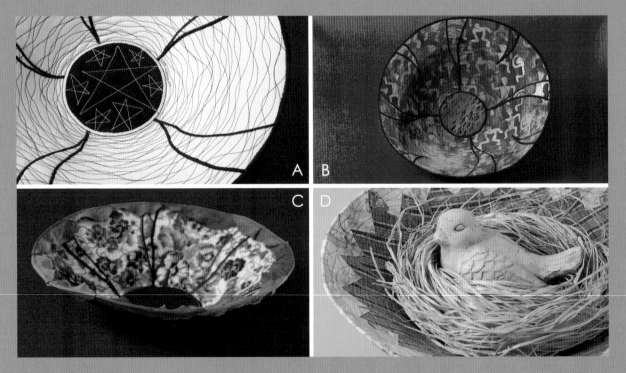

hexagon bowl

Create either of two hexagonal shapes—one with each edge straight, the other with pointed edges. In either case, choose hex-citing fabrics, such as the unexpected flannels shown here or fun and funky theme prints.

What You'll Need

- 2 fat quarters of complementary fabrics
- 5" scraps of accent fabrics, for bases
- 1 yard of fusible web
- 1 package, or ½ yard Timtex for the stabilizer (see page 8 for a substitute)
- Thread to match or contrast
- Large sheet of newsprint paper for pattern
- Large, clear quilter's rulers: rectangular ruler with a marked 60° line; square ruler 12½" or larger
- Basic supplies (see pages 9–11)

How-To's
making the patterns

1. Using the square ruler, measure and cut a 10" x 12" rectangle of paper. Fold the paper lengthwise in half so that it measures 5" x 12", and place it on a cutting mat.

2. Align the 60° line of a rectangular quilter's ruler on the fold as shown. Cut along the long edge of the ruler.

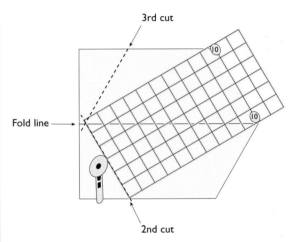

Make the second and third cuts 10" away from the first cut.

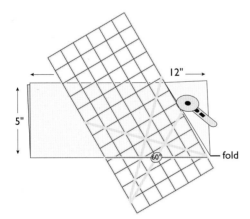

With the 60° line along the fold, cut along the long edge.

3. Unfold the paper, then make cuts 10" from each of the edges you just cut.

4. For the base pattern, start with a 3" x 5" piece of paper, or index card. Referring to Steps 2 and 3 above, fold it lengthwise in half, cut a 60° angle, then make cuts so the finished hexagon measures 3" from one side to the other.

easy!

You can use a 3" round base instead of a hexagonal base. The centering and dart-making will be exactly the same.

making the textile sandwich

1. Place the paper pattern for the 10" hexagon on Timtex, securing with tape. Align a rotary ruler with each side of the hexagon pattern, and rotary-cut a Timtex hexagon.

2. Stack 2 fabrics and 2 layers of fusible web. Place the 10" Timtex hexagon on top of the stack and rotary-cut ½" larger all around than the Timtex.

3. Press fusible web to the wrong side of each fabric hexagon. Center 1 large fusible-backed fabric on the Timtex, and press to fuse. Use a rotary cutter and ruler to trim each side even with the Timtex. Fuse fabric to the other side of the Timtex, and trim the edges.

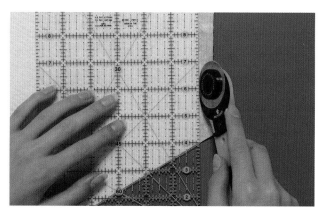

Trim edges even with the Timtex.

fun! Fold the paper backing from the fusible into six "pie" wedges. Use each wedge as a pattern to cut a different fabric for each side panel of the bowl. Fuse each wedge in place.

adding the bases

1. Apply fusible web to the wrong side of 2 pieces of fabric, each about 5" square. Cut out 2 bases, using the 3" hexagon paper pattern.

2. Use a ruler to draw 1 set of lines—*either* for Option A *or* for Option B. Work on either side of the textile sandwich, using any marking tool that will show up.

Option A: Straight Edges from Dart to Dart

Using a ruler, draw 3 guidelines, each connecting opposite corners and crossing the center of the textile sandwich.

Option B: Pointed Edges Between Darts

Measure and mark the midpoint of each edge of the hexagonal textile sandwich. Using a ruler, draw 3 guidelines, each connecting opposite midpoints and crossing the center of the textile sandwich.

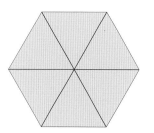 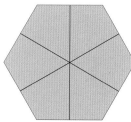

Guidelines for Option A   Guidelines for Option B

3. With either option, place one 3" hexagon base with each corner on a line. Press to fuse it in place.

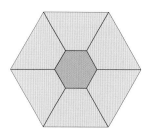 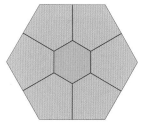

Positioning the Base for   Positioning the Base for
Option A   Option B

4. Straight stitch just outside the edges of the base. Sew as close as possible to the base, but not on it. Flip the textile sandwich to the other side, and position the second fusible-backed fabric hexagon inside the stitching. Press to fuse this piece in place.

5. Use some scraps similar to the textile sandwich to check your stitches and tension before you begin stitching on your bowl. Using a medium-width satin stitch, sew around the edge of the base once or twice, until it looks finished to you. As you sew, keep the center of the satin stitch along the edge of the base.

shaping the bowl

1. Mark points at the edge of the textile sandwich, ½" to either side of each guideline you marked across the center of the sandwich.

2. Connect these marks to a point ⅛" from the corner of the base. Draw in all the darts before you begin to cut them out and stitch them.

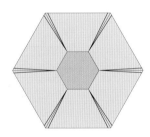 

Marked Darts for Option A   Marked Darts for Option B

3. Cut along the 2 marked lines, and remove 1 dart only. *Sharp* scissors really help here!

4. Set your machine for a medium satin stitch, and use the cut-out dart piece as a scrap to check the stitches and tension. Place the needle of your machine exactly at one corner of the base, with the cut-out dart in front of the needle. Sew a few satin stitches, then backstitch to anchor the thread.

Begin stitching the dart at the base.

5. Continue satin stitching toward the edge of the textile sandwich. As you sew, pull the edges of the dart together in front of the needle, so the zigzag stitch catches both edges equally. Work slowly—if you try to pull the whole dart together when you start, you'll have puckering at the base of your dart. Stop when you reach the edge, and don't backstitch, because satin stitching along the edge will secure these threads later.

6. Cut and stitch the remaining 5 darts the same way. For a more finished look, go over each dart again, using a slightly wider satin stitch.

finishing

1. If necessary, use small, sharp scissors to trim the textile sandwich on either side of the dart so that the edges meet perfectly at the dart.

2. Satin stitch around the edge of the bowl, using the same setting. You want the right side of the satin stitch to consistently fall just beyond the edge of the fabric. Make a second round using a slightly wider satin stitch. Finish off with lock-stitches.

Hex-cellent **results** either way, and, of course, each is **reversible!**

Variations

Novelty fabrics and conversation prints will inspire you to make a different version of this bowl for each season of the year.

A. For fall, use Halloween fabrics and fill your bowl with some candy corn for trick-or-treaters of all ages.

B. The pointy version of this design brings pointy-petalled poinsettias and Christmas to mind, inspiring a bowl for everyone on your gift list.

C. Symbolize the freshness of spring with a floral or a barnyard print. This bowl starts from a 12" <u>circle</u>, but the rest of the process is the same.

D. Show your patriotism on the Fourth of July—or anytime!—with flag prints, adding buttons along the rim.

triangle bowl

Sawtooth edging, fin-like darts, and the chance to flip, fold, and play with this shape, all make this bowl loads of fun—from any angle!

What You'll Need

- 3 fat quarters: 1 for the base and edging squares, plus 2 different, complementary fabrics
- ½ yard of unwashed heavy weight canvas (see page 8)
- 1 yard of fusible web
- Thread to match or contrast
- Round dinner plate
- Compass
- 80/12 topstitch needle
- Basic supplies (see pages 9–11)

How-To's

making the textile sandwich

1. Stack 1 layer of canvas, 2 layers of fabric right sides together, and 2 layers of fusible web face to face.

2. Referring to the Round Bowl how-to's for Making the Textile Sandwich on page 21, measure, mark, and cut a 14" circle. Press to fuse web to the wrong side of each fabric, peel away the paper backing, and fuse the fabric circles to either side of the canvas.

3. Trim the textile sandwich so it's as round as possible. Any exposed canvas will be covered with sawtooth squares.

4. Starting at the center of the textile sandwich and ending at the outer edge, straight-stitch in a wavy, random spiral. Refer to the how-to's for Quilting the Surface, Step 2, page 23. No need for dense stitching—you will be doing more spiral stitching after you add the sawtooth edging.

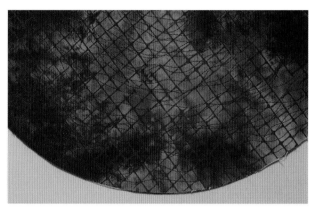

Quilt in a wavy, random spiral.

adding the base

1. Roughly cut out 5" high equilateral triangles: 2 from fabric and 2 from canvas. Iron fusible web to the back of each piece. Use the patterns on page 35 to cut out 2 triangles 4¼" in height from canvas and 2 triangles 4½" in height from fabric.

easy! An equilateral (60°) template such as the Clearview Triangle™ ruler by Sara Nephew works perfectly as a template.

2. Move the pieces to an ironing surface. Remove the paper backings. Lay 1 canvas triangle on the textile sandwich. Center it by measuring from each corner of the triangle base to the edge of the bowl. Fuse it in place.

3. Straight stitch along the edge of the canvas, as close as possible to the base but not on it.

Stitch a guideline for positioning the other canvas base.

4. Turn the textile sandwich over, position the second canvas base within the stitched lines, and then fuse the base in place.

5. Center a fabric triangle base over each canvas base, and fuse it in place.

6. If desired, quilt the base, using a straight stitch and decorative thread. Consider a spiral of concentric triangles or a more complex, free-motion pattern (see page 39).

Design Possibilities for the Base

7. Satin stitch around the edge of the base, covering the raw edges. If the stitches don't cover the edge of the base on the reverse side, restitch with a wider satin stitch.

sawtooth edging

1. From the same fabric used for the base, cut a 12" x 8" piece of fabric.

2. Apply fusible web to the back of the fabric, remove the paper backing, and then cut it into 2" squares.

fast! Instead of fusing, apply a light coat of temporary basting spray. There'll be no ironing necessary from here on in!

3. Work on an ironing surface protected with a non-stick pressing sheet. Place each small square along the edge of the bowl, so that 2 opposite points are along the edge. Overlap squares by about ¾", and when you get to the last square, tuck it under the first one.

Overlap small squares all around the edge.

4. Press the small squares in place. Flip the textile sandwich and tug a little on the squares as you press them in place on the second side.

5. Sew wavy lines around the edge to better secure the edges of the small squares. Use this opportunity to add more spirals around the bowl, because after you sew the darts you won't be able to add any more stitching.

Secure the small squares with more stitching.

making the darts

1. Your first darts will be at the 3 corners of the base. Fold the textile sandwich from one corner of the base to the edge, for an outward dart. Insert a pin straight into the textile sandwich, along this fold and 2¾" from the outer edge.

2. Begin straight stitching the dart at the edge of the textile sandwich, ½" from the fold. Make a few backstitches, then head straight toward the pin. Backstitch at the end of the dart.

3. Repeat Steps 1 and 2 at each corner of the base for a total of 3 outward darts.

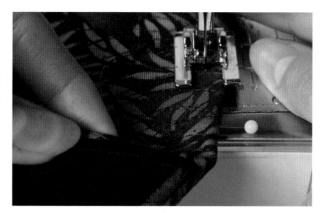

Stitch the dart.

4. Flip the bowl to the reverse side. Find the center of the sides between 2 darts by lining up 2 darts and pinching the fabric. Pin and sew, using the same measurements as before. Repeat this step on all 3 sides of the bowl to make a total of 3 inward darts. *Note:* Because the second set of darts starts farther away from the base than the first set, they *seem* shorter than the first 3 darts, but they really aren't!

4¼"

4½"

Actual-Size Patterns for Base Pieces

Now **your bowl** features a very **sculptural,** versatile shape!

Variations

With a little play-time, you can change the look completely, or merely manipulate the shape of the bowl. "Tri" these ideas on for size:

A. Place the corner darts on the outside of the bowl and push in the side darts. Voila! a three-sided bowl.

B. To get a fresh, flower shape, make all the darts face inward.

C. Changing the shape of the sawtooth edging from 2" squares to 2" diamonds gives the bowl even more drama.

D. Skip the sawtooth edging altogether! Before creating the darts, finish the edge with satin stitching.

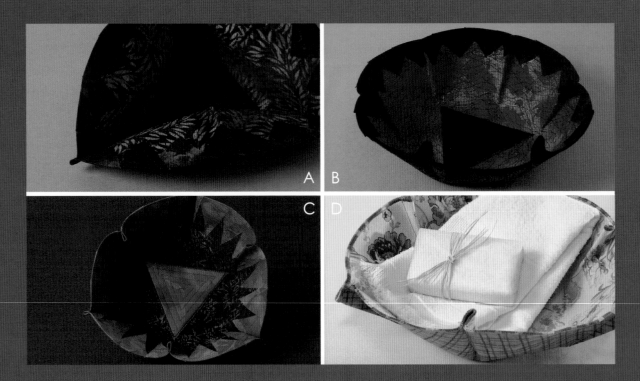

octagon bowl

Don't let the elegant look fool you—
eight darts cut along a circle, lead
effortlessly to a rich, ribbed texture
and a graceful, scalloped edge.

What You'll Need

- ☐ 2 fat quarters of complementary fabrics
- ☐ 4½" scraps of accent fabrics
- ☐ 1 yard of fusible web
- ☐ 1 package, or ½ yard of Timtex for the stabilizer (see page 8 for a substitute)
- ☐ Thread to match or contrast
- ☐ Serving plate, 13" in diameter, or large dinner plate and compass
- ☐ Quilter's ruler at least 18" long, with a marked 45° angle
- ☐ Template plastic or tracing paper
- ☐ Basic supplies (see pages 9–11)

How-To's

making the textile sandwich

1. Use a round plate, and a compass if necessary, to cut a 13" diameter circle from Timtex. See page 21 for complete how-to's.

2. Using the Timtex as a pattern, cut out circles ½" larger all around: 1 from each fabric, and 2 from fusible web. Press a fusible web circle to the wrong side of each fabric circle.

3. Remove the paper backing from both large fabric circles. Protect your ironing surface with a pressing sheet. Fuse 1 fabric circle to the Timtex. Let cool, then trim the edges even with the Timtex. Repeat to fuse a fabric circle to the other side, and trim the edges even.

marking 8 division lines

1. Using a long quilter's ruler with a marked 45°, locate the exact center of the textile sandwich, and mark with a dot.

2. Draw a line across the exact center of the circle. Draw a second line at a 90° angle to the first.

3. Draw a third line at a 45° angle to one of the first 2 lines. Draw a fourth line at a 90° angle to the last line drawn. You should have 8 even sections marked.

adding the bases

1. Apply fusible web to the wrong side of 2 pieces (or scraps) of fabric, each at least 4½" square. On the paper backing of one of the pieces, draw a 3½" circle with a compass. Cut it out with scissors; don't mark or cut the second piece yet.

2. To find the center of the 3½" base, fold it into quarters with the paper backing on the inside, and lightly crease the point. Unfold and insert a pin up through the circle, from the fabric side, at the center point. Remove the paper backing from the fusible web.

3. Insert the pin into the center of the textile sandwich, where all the lines cross. Press to fuse the base in place.

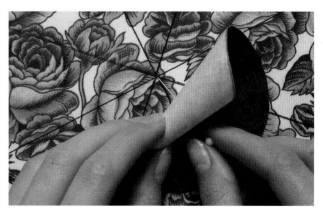

Center the base on the textile sandwich.

4. Peel away the paper from the second fabric scrap and center it on the reverse side of the textile sandwich. Peek under the sandwich to make sure it covers the same area that the first base occupies. Apply basting spray to temporarily hold it in place.

5. Using a slightly shortened stitch length, straight stitch around the smaller base, keeping stitches ⅟16" to the inside of the edge. Flip the textile sandwich and trim away the excess fabric beyond the stitches. See the top left photo on page 23.

Satin stitch around the base.

easy! Double curved appliqué scissors make close trimming a cinch to do.

fun! This bowl does not need any stitching to firm up the base, but consider adding some decorative quilting anyway!

6. Press to fuse the second base in place. Check your stitches and tension on a scrap of layered materials, then sew a medium-width satin stitch around the edge of the base.

marking and cutting darts

1. Photocopy or trace templates A and B. Cut them out from paper or template plastic, and mark the center line with a ruler.

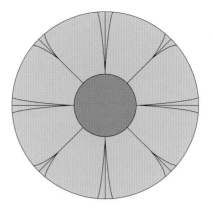

Mark the darts, alternating A and B templates.

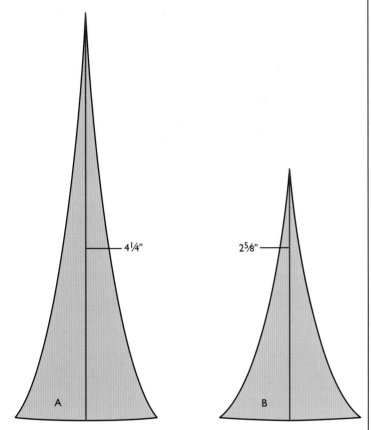

— 4¼" —

— 2⅝" —

A

B

Actual-Size Template Patterns for Darts

2. Place the center line of one template on a marked division line, matching the outer edges. Trace along both long edges of the template. Repeat this step around the circle, alternating templates A and B for long and short darts. Mark all the darts before cutting and sewing.

shaping the bowl

1. Cut along the 2 marked lines of a long A dart, and remove the dart. Cut with sharp scissors, and cut only one dart at a time just before you sew, so there's less opportunity for the fabric to fray.

Cut and stitch 1 dart at a time.

2. Use a medium-width satin stitch, and check your stitches and tension on a cut-out dart. Place the needle of your machine exactly at the edge of the base, with the cut edges of an A dart in front of the needle. Sew a few stitches, backstitch to anchor the thread, and then continue toward the edge of the textile sandwich. As you sew, pull the edges of the dart together to meet just in front of the needle, and keep the zigzag stitch centered over both edges. Work slowly and carefully. If you try to pull the whole dart together when you start, you'll have puckering at the base of your dart.

3. The bowl will begin to curve a lot more as you get close to the rim. At this point, you will need to pull quite firmly. Continue stitching to the edge of the textile sandwich. No need to backstitch—satin stitching along the edge will take care of catching these threads later.

4. Next, satin stitch a shorter B dart. Again, begin sewing at the edge of the base, and sew along the entire marked line, as if you had cut it all the way to the base. In this way, cut and sew all the darts as you come to them. When that is done, go over each dart a second time, using a slightly wider satin stitch. Backstitch at the beginning to anchor the thread.

Sew along the entire marked line of a B dart.

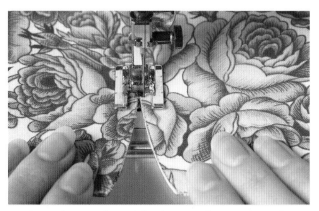
Bring the cut edges of the dart together as you stitch.

finishing

1. The edges of your bowl should form gentle, even scallops. If they don't, use a pair of sharp scissors to carefully trim the high edge to meet the lower one.

2. Sew around the edge of the bowl with a medium-width satin stitch. You want the right side of the satin stitch to consistently fall just beyond the edge of the fabric. Pivot at each dart to make a crisp angle.

3. Repeat, using a slightly wider satin stitch. Finish off with lock-stitches.

fun!

For a very different bowl, mark and cut straight darts.

Why not make an
octagon bowl
for any friend or relative
with the good taste to
appreciate such a
classy gift?

Variations

The graceful lines of this bowl enable you to dress it up or down.

A. For a softer, more casual appeal, use a canvas stabilizer instead of Timtex. Heavy denim does dual-duty as outer fabric and stabilizer.

B. For a feminine, garden-party look, choose a floral print. Trace around the edge of a teacup to make the scallops rounder and deeper.

C. Add sophistication by draping beaded fringe around the edges. Stitch in place.

D. If you're after a contemporary, angular shape, use a ruler to draw the darts, straightening the curves of the templates. See the same bowl vamped up with a feather boa effect on the opposite page!

A B
C D

fun with embellishments

Comfortable with the basics of bowl-making? Then it's time for a little adventure. Here are a few ways to add touches of creativity, whimsy, elegance, or unique personality to your beautiful bowl!

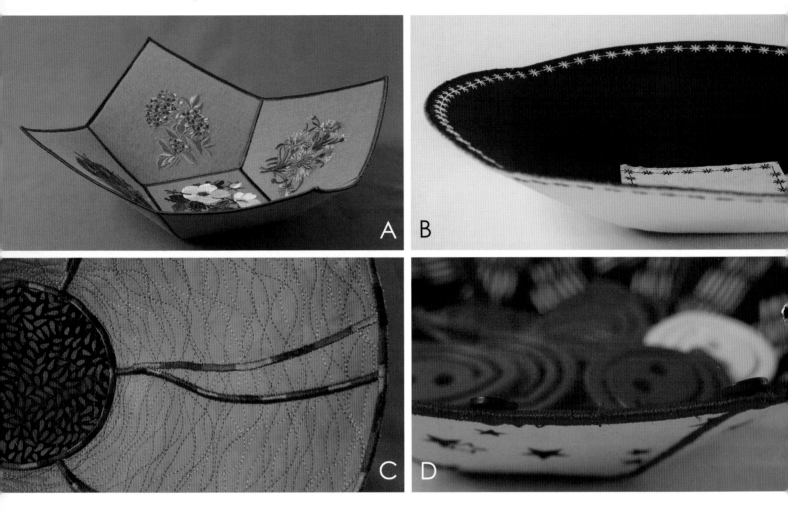

A. Embroidery Use embroidered fabric on one side of your bowl. Or if you have an embroidery machine, create your own fabric, as Marta Alto did here.

B. Decorative Stitches Accent your bowl with decorative stitches. Decorate the base of the bowl while the textile sandwich is still flat. Adorn the rim for a finishing touch.

C. Thread Add excitement to the satin stitching around the base, along the darts, and/or along the rim by using variegated thread in the top of the machine. Use a solid, matching thread for the bobbin.

D. Buttons Sew buttons, using an embroidery needle to pierce through all of the layers, along the rim of your bowl. You can space a few buttons at the points or darts, or encircle the entire rim.

E. Chenille Create chenille edging for your bowl. Cut bias strips of fabric and sew them around the edge on both sides of the bowl. Launder the bowl to unravel the fabric, which will create a chenille edge.

F. Novelty Trim Decorate the rim of your bowl with novelty trims like the loopy yarn shown here. First finish the edge of the bowl with satin stitches. Then use the same thread, or a monofilament thread, to zigzag stitch to catch the edge of the trim.

G. Beaded Fringe Finish the edge of the bowl and then use the same thread, or a monofilament thread, to add beads or a beaded fringe. Zigzag stitch along both edges of the trim.

H. "Feather Boa" Finish the edge of the bowl with satin stitches. Then use the same thread, to couch a lush, fringey yarn in place.

I. Silk Leaves and Flowers Cultivate a garden look for your bowl by adding silk leaves and flowers. Remove any plastic stems or veins from the silk leaves. Fold the leaves over the edge of the bowl and use a straight stitch along the edge to hold the leaves in place. Sew on individual flowers by hand or machine.

J. Hidden Darts Cover up the dart edges by fusing the same fabric over them. Apply a sawtooth edging (see page 34) and lots of spiral stitching.

K. Sawtooth Edging This design detail can be added to any bowl after it has been shaped, and is a great way to finish the rim.

L. Tall Peaks For a deep sawtooth edge, start with 45° or 60° diamonds. See page 34 for how-to's.

troubleshooting tips

Problem: I don't like the way the base of my bowl looks.

Solution: At any point (even if the rest of the bowl is finished) you can cut a new base, back the fabric with fusible web, and iron it over the existing base. Choose a different fabric, or cover stitching that didn't work. Finish the edges with satin stitching.

Problem: I made a mistake cutting the dart.

Solutions: A. Rip it out and redo it, making more or less of an overlap. B. Trim the overlapped dart before you sew the second side. C. If you've removed a dart, consider sewing a narrower dart back into the bowl. D. Make more darts with the same "mistake"!

Problem: The threads show through on the other side of the bowl.

Solution: If you are having trouble with the thread on the top of your piece, check your bobbin tension and threading. If the trouble is extra thread on the underside, check your top tension and threading. For satin stitching, check to see if the arm on your bobbin case has a little hole. If it does, pass the bobbin thread through it.

Problem: My satin stitch produces big bumps of thread when I pivot to change direction.

Solution: At the corners, lift the presser foot slightly to help the bowl through, or put a scrap of the bowl sandwich under the back of the presser foot. As you overlap stitches, increase your stitch length slightly.

Problem: My needles keep breaking.

Solution: Try a larger-size needle. Let your machine do the work. Don't try to "muscle" the project. Gentle pulling may help sometimes, but if you pull when the needle is down, it will break.

free-motion quilting

Proper machine set-up and lots of practice are the secrets to success.

1. Lower the feed dogs on your machine. If your sewing machine doesn't have feed dogs that lower, then cover them with an index card, taped over the feed dog slots.

2. Attach a darning foot to your machine. This foot clamps the textile sandwich in place when the needle is down, but releases the textile sandwich when the needle is up. You have the freedom to move the fabric in any direction while the needle is up.

3. Decrease or loosen the presser foot and upper thread tension.

4. Practice on a test sandwich similar to your fabric bowl—or on the textile sandwich that will become your fabric bowl. Move the sandwich in all directions, making straight lines, curves, or meander stitches. Adjust the tension by tiny amounts until you achieve a balanced stitch—even on both sides. Use consistent speed, for the machine and moving the fabric, to produce stitches that are the same length throughout.

About the Author

When Linda was seven years old, her mother sat her down at a treadle sewing machine and taught her how to sew. By the time she was in junior high school, she was making all her own clothes. She loves to stretch her creativity with every innovative fabric technique she can find, from dyeing, painting, and stamping, to making bowls. And as of this writing, she has created over 200 bowls!

Linda teaches workshops on beginning, traditional, and contemporary quiltmaking; color and design; dyeing and stamping. Of course, her very popular class on making fabric bowls is always filled. Under the company name Johansen Dyeworks, Linda hand-dyes fabric, specializing in color gradations and variegated, one-of-a-kind pieces. This fabric, along with commissioned art quilts and fabric bowls, are sold through several shops around the Northwest.

Although her two sons have grown up and left the nest, Linda still has the company of two border collie mix dogs. She and her husband live in Corvallis, Oregon.

Sources

For materials and tools mentioned in this book, check your local quilt shop or try the following mail-order sources.

Timtex™: 22" wide yardage; a bolt holds 10 yards

Timber Lane Press (Timtex™ is made exclusively for this company; will take wholesale orders or recommend retail outlets)
24350 N. Rimrock Road
Hayden, ID 83835
(208) 765-3353
(800) 752-3353 wholesale orders only
Email: qltblox@earthlink.net

Clotilde LLC (Timtex™ sold in package 13½" x 22"; assorted tools and fabrics)
P.O. Box 7500
Big Sandy, TX 75755-7500
(800) 772-2891
Website: www.clotilde.com

A Common Thread (Timtex™ yardage; Clearview Triangle, and other assorted tools and fabrics)
16925 SW 65th
Lake Oswego, OR 97035
(877) 915-6789 (toll free)
Email: actbernina@aol.com
Website:
www.acommonthreadfabrics.com

Log Cabin Dry Goods
3607 East French Gulch Road
Coeur d'Alene, ID 83814
(208) 664-5908
Email: logcabindrygoods@mindspring.com
Website: www.logcabindrygoods.com

Also available through major quilting supply distributors

Other Supplies:

Clearview Triangle (equilateral triangle ruler)
8311 180th St SE
Snohomish, WA 98296-4802
(888) 901-4151

Johansen Dyeworks (hand dyed fabrics)
465 SE Bridgeway Ave.
Corvallis, OR 97333
Email: jthatch@peak.org

For a list of other fine books by C&T Publishing, write for a free catalog:
C&T Publishing, Inc. • P.O. Box 1456 • Lafayette, CA 94549 • (800) 284-1114 • Email: ctinfo@ctpub.com • Website: www.ctpub.com

For general quilting supplies:
Cotton Patch Mail Order • 3405 Hall Lane, Dept.CTB • Lafayette, CA 94549 • (800) 835-4418 • (925) 283-7883 •
Email:quiltusa@yahoo.com • Website: www.quiltusa.com